D0576792

Guess What

Published in the United States of America by
Cherry Lake Publishing
Ann Arbor, Michigan
www.cherrylakepublishing.com

Content Adviser: Susan Heinrichs Gray
Reading Adviser: Marla Conn, ReadAbility, Inc.
Book Designer: Felicia Macheske

Photo Credits: © QiuJu Song/Shutterstock Images, cover, 3, 14; Stubblefield Photography/Shutterstock Images, 1; © Kerry L. Werry/Shutterstock Images, 4; Ethan Daniels/Shutterstock Images, 7; Dieter Hawlan/Shutterstock Images, 9; Ye Choh Wah/Shutterstock Images, 10; Vittorio Bruno/Shutterstock Images, 13; Evikka/Shutterstock Images, 17; nudiblue/Shutterstock Images, 18; Rich Carey/Shutterstock Images, 21; © Andrey_Kuzmin/Shutterstock Images, back cover; © Eric Isselee/Shutterstock Images, back cover

Library of Congress Cataloging-in-Publication Data

Macheske, Felicia, author.
 Awesome arms / Felicia Macheske.
 pages cm. — (Guess what)
 Summary: "Young children are natural problem solvers and always looking for answers, especially when it involves ocean animals. Guess What: Awesome Arms: Octopus provides young curious readers with striking visual clues and simply written hints. Using the photos and text, readers rely on visual literacy skills, reading, and reasoning as they solve the animal mystery. Clearly written facts give readers a deeper understanding of how the octopus lives. Additional text features, including a glossary and an index, help students locate information and learn new words"— Provided by publisher.
 Audience: K to grade 3.
 Includes index.
 ISBN 978-1-63470-718-3 (hardcover) — ISBN 978-1-63470-733-6 (pdf) — ISBN 978-1-63470-748-0 (pbk.) — ISBN 978-1-63470-763-3 (ebook)
 1. Octopuses—Juvenile literature. 2. Children's questions and answers. I. Title.
 QL430.3.O2M33 2016
 594'.56—dc23
 2015026120

Cherry Lake Publishing would like to acknowledge the work of The Partnership for 21st Century Skills.
Please visit *www.p21.org* for more information.

Printed in the United States of America
Corporate Graphics

Table of Contents

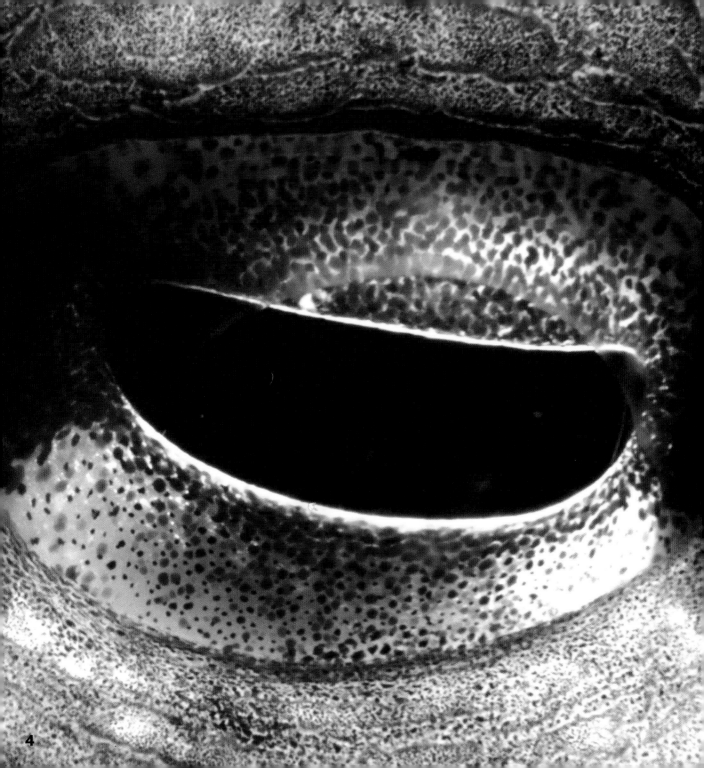

I have good eyesight.

I can change color and shape.

I have a **tube** that helps me swim.

I can squeeze into very small places.

I use **ink** to **hide** myself.

13

I have eight long arms.

The suckers on my arms can taste things.

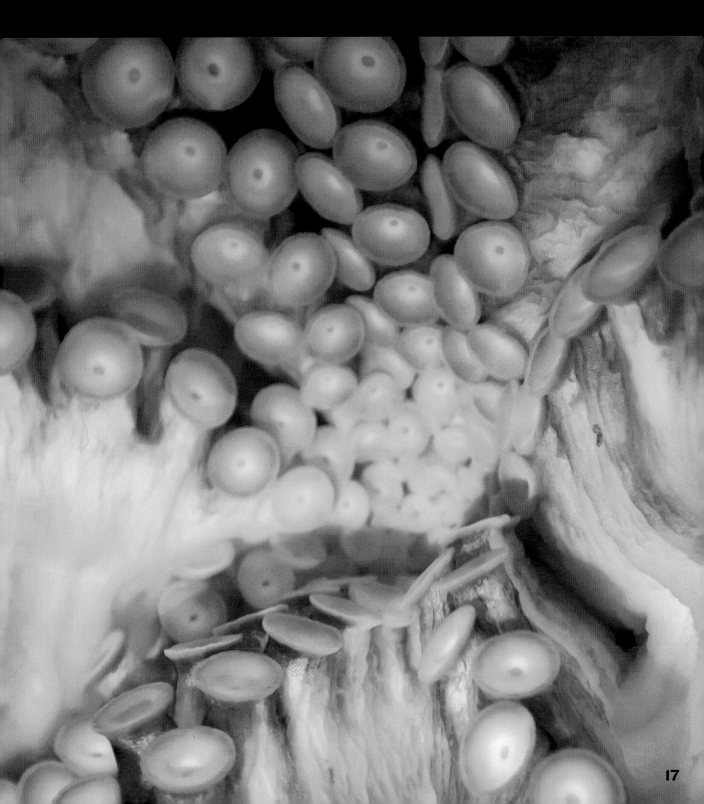

I live in the ocean.

Do you know what I am?

I'm an Octopus!

About Octopuses

1. Octopuses have a **beak** that they use to eat food.

2. Octopuses are very smart. They seem to use tools and play with toys.

3. Octopuses live only three to five years.

4. The suckers on an octopus's arms can taste and feel things.

5. An octopus can lose an arm and grow a new one.

Glossary

beak (BEEK) the hard, pointed jaw of an animal

eyesight (EYE-site) the ability to see

ink (INGK) a colored liquid that octopuses can squirt

tube (TOOB) a hollow, circular body part used for pushing water

squeeze (SKWEEZ) to barely get into or through a space

suckers (SUHK-urz) the body parts of some animals that are used to stick to surfaces

Index